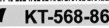

Planning for a
SUSTAINABLE
FUTURE

WITHDRAWN

Th...k i   before the

Helen Belmont

FRANKLIN WATTS

First published in 2007 by

Franklin Watts

338 Euston Road

London NW1 3BH

Franklin Watts Australia

Hachette Children's Books

Level 17/207 Kent Street

Sydney NSW 2000

Copyright © Franklin Watts 2007

Editor: Jennifer Schofield

Consultant: Steve Watts
(FRGS, Principal Lecturer University of Sunderland)

Art director: Jonathan Hair

Design: Mo Choy

Artwork: John Alston

Picture researcher: Kathy Lockley

Acknowledgements

© Alfred d'Amato/Panos Pictures 40. Art Directors & TRIP Photo Library 13, 38. Ross Barnett/Lonely Planet Images 35.

Sarah Clifford, Piedra Blanca Community EcoTourism Project. www.piedrablanca.org 37. Neil Cooper/Still Pictures 11.

Nigel Dickenson/Still Pictures 41. © Digital Vision COVER, 3, 9, 17, © Natalie Forbes/Corbis 39. Courtesy of the Grameen Foundation 43.

Chris Fairclough 24. Jeff Greenberg/Lonely Planet Images 28. Robert Harding Picture Library 18, 31, 36. © Collart Herve/Corbis Sygma 7.

Daniel Heuclin/NHPA 15. © Ed Quinn/Corbis 34. © Roger Ressmeyer/Corbis 23. © Karen Robinson/Panos Pictures 32. Jorgen Schytte/

Still Pictures 10. Jonathan & Angela Scott/NHPA 8. Sean Sprague/Still Pictures 27. Volker Steger/Science Photo Library 42.

Manfred Vollmer/Still Pictures 19. ©. Phillip Walmuth/Panos Pictures 6.

Every attempt has been made to clear copyright.
Should there be any inadvertent omission please
apply to the publisher for rectification.

A CIP catalogue record for this book
is available from the British Library.

ISBN-10: 0 7496 6785 0

ISBN-13: 978 0 7496 6785 6

Dewey Classification: 551.41

Printed in China

Franklin Watts is a division of Hachette Children's Books.

Contents

Planning for the future

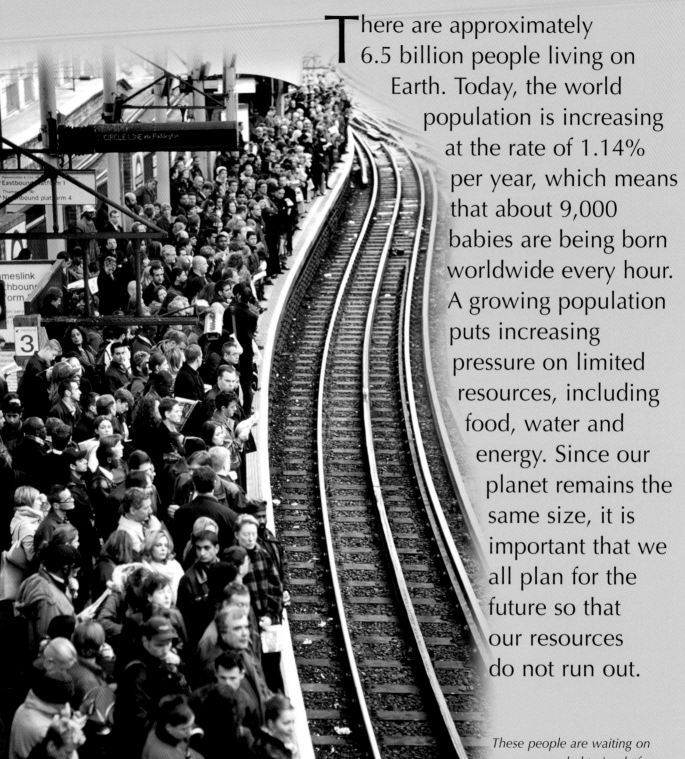

There are approximately 6.5 billion people living on Earth. Today, the world population is increasing at the rate of 1.14% per year, which means that about 9,000 babies are being born worldwide every hour. A growing population puts increasing pressure on limited resources, including food, water and energy. Since our planet remains the same size, it is important that we all plan for the future so that our resources do not run out.

These people are waiting on an overcrowded train platform. How will we get around in the future when there are even more people who want to travel?

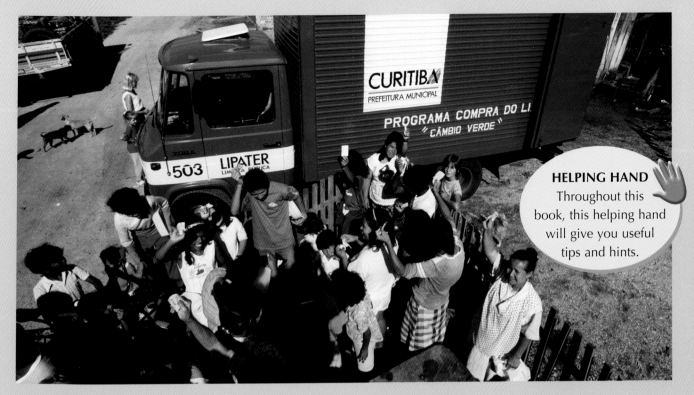

HELPING HAND
Throughout this book, this helping hand will give you useful tips and hints.

STEWARDSHIP

As individuals, we are all stewards of our planet. This means we are its guardians, caring for it today and leaving it in a good condition for future generations. We can do this by thinking about the way we use Earth's resources, such as oil and metals, water and wood, day-to-day.

NATIONAL AND INTERNATIONAL STEWARDSHIP

People in government can make laws to protect the environment and to encourage people to become good stewards. This can also be done at an international level.

The first international Earth Summit was held in 1992 in Rio de Janeiro, Brazil. At this meeting, and at others since, representatives from all over the world discussed the condition of the planet. They have agreed on a number of steps that countries could take to help Earth stay healthy, in response to concerns about damage caused by pollution and the use of too many natural resources.

People today must be responsible for keeping our planet healthy – even if they need to be encouraged. These people in Curitiba, Brazil (see page 31) are swapping their rubbish for bus tickets.

WARNING SIGN
When you see this sign, you should be extra careful when completing the task.

KEY SKILLS

Throughout this book, you will learn different skills. Each different skill is represented by one of the following icons:

 Completing a practical activity

 Analysing information

 Working with graphs, maps, diagrams and photographs

 Looking at global issues

 Researching information

 Observing

What is sustainability?

Sustainability is about living in a way that does not damage Earth for future generations. At the Rio Earth Summit (see page 7) and later meetings, politicians discussed how well each country is managing to work towards a sustainable future.

(see page 7)

KEY SKILLS

Using the Internet

Filling in a questionnaire

Interpreting results

GETTING THE BALANCE RIGHT

Sustainability can be broken down into different categories, depending on how humans are using Earth's resources with regard to the environment and sustainability. The three categories are:

1) Environmental sustainability – protecting the environment (including wildlife, landscape and Earth's resources) from pollution and overuse.

2) Social justice – ensuring people have a good quality of life. It is also about people being able to maintain a quality of life without jeopardising Earth's resources.
3) Economic well-being – ensuring that people can reach a decent quality of life through work without overusing Earth's resources and putting the planet in danger.

To achieve sustainability, people need to implement all three categories.

These giraffes are on the African plains. Protecting natural environments is one of the three categories of sustainability.

ECO FOOTPRINT

We can measure how sustainable our own lives are by calculating the size of our eco footprint. The footprint is the amount of productive land and sea needed to sustain a person's lifestyle – the amount of food they eat, the products that they use and discard and the amount of energy they use every day. Eco footprints vary tremendously across nations. For example in the UK, the average footprint is 5.35 global hectares, while in Mozambique it is 0.47 global hectares. Today, there is only enough productive area on Earth for us each to have 1.9 global hectares.

A power station in the United States of America. We all use electricity and other sources of power. How much we use is reflected in our eco footprint.

MEASURE YOUR ECO FOOTPRINT

To measure your eco footprint go to www.ecofoot.com and click on 'your footprint'. Fill in some of the questions; you may need help from a parent, carer or teacher. Work out your eco footprint and then look at what you could do to reduce it. The higher the number the bigger your negative impact on the Earth.

Water – a key resource

Water is essential for life. We use it in so many ways: for transport, in industry and agriculture, to keep our bodies and clothes clean, and to drink. Unfortunately, water is not distributed evenly across the world and many places in less economically developed countries (LEDCs) do not have clean water. So how should we plan for everyone to have clean drinking water in the future?

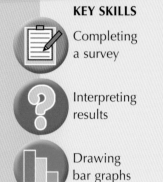

KEY SKILLS

Completing a survey

Interpreting results

Drawing bar graphs

HEALTH EDUCATION

Farmers in some areas of the world need flood water to grow crops, but too much can cause death and destruction. During a flood, drinking water can become polluted with sewage and engine oil. In some countries, such as Bangladesh where areas are often flooded, the government and aid charities are working with local people to teach them about healthcare. They give out water purification tablets that are used to clean small amounts of water. They dig special wells to try to reduce the contamination of drinking water.

A water education class in Bangladesh. Children are taught where to collect safe water, and what to do after a flood.

DIGGING MORE WELLS

In countries such as Malawi in Africa, there is so little rainfall that many people spend up to three hours a day walking to wells or rivers to collect water for their family. Not only is this extremely hard work but also it leaves them little time to do anything else. Is this sustainable? Slowly governments and charities are working to dig wells closer to where people live. One charity recently dug 33 wells to supply clean water to 100,000 people in Malawian villages.

Engineers dig a well in Kenya. Wells provide villages with a clean source of water – something that many people take for granted.

WATER QUESTIONNAIRE

You are going to do a survey on how your friends and family use water. Start by drawing up a questionnaire similar to the one on the right. Group your answers together and represent them using a bar graph. Find out which actions use least water and encourage people to save water. Repeat the questionnaire at a later date to see how your results have changed.

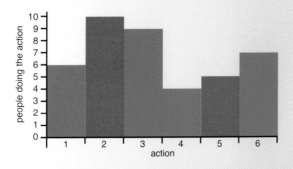

ACTION	YES	NO
1. Do you leave the tap running while you brush your teeth?		
2. Do you take a shower?		
3. Do you take a bath?		
4. Do you use a hosepipe to clean the car?		
5. Do you use a bucket and sponge to clean the car?		
6. Do you run the washing machine with a full load each time?		

River planning

River systems are part of the water cycle, transferring rain from the drainage basin and eventually carrying it to the ocean. People use rivers for transporting goods, for irrigating crops, for creating reservoirs of fresh water to turn into drinking water and for hydro-electricity. Geographers are often asked to become involved in making plans for managing rivers in the future.

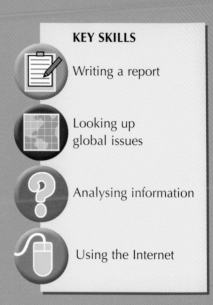

KEY SKILLS

Writing a report

Looking up global issues

Analysing information

Using the Internet

INVESTIGATING RIVER USE

Some rivers are enormous and bring vital water to whole countries. Look up the River Nile in Egypt in an atlas to see its size and extent. Use the Internet to find out how important the river is to the people of Egypt. Find out about the Aswan Dam and the effect it is having on the River Nile and the surrounding area.

USING THE FLOODPLAIN

The flat land either side of a river is called the floodplain. When the river floods, fertile sediment (mud) carried in the river water is deposited on the floodplain, making the land very fertile (good for growing crops). In addition, because the land is flat, it makes perfect building land for houses and industries.

To use more of the land, farmers and land developers often drain some of the floodplain and alter the course of the river to make it safer and easier to use. In some places huge banks are built up to prevent the river from flooding onto the surrounding land. Dams and barriers help to prevent flooding, too. These changes also have other, unwanted effects. The wildlife of the river can be changed by building work and some types of river plant and animal life may gradually disappear from the area. Sediment collects behind dams and barriers and does not flow onto floodplains. As a result, the nutrient-rich mud that the river carries does not fertilise the land.

HOLISTIC PLANNING

While traditional river planning continues in many places, the way forward is thought to be holistic planning. This means thinking about the whole river over a whole year, not just one place for a few months.

RESEARCH AND REPORT

The River Brede in Denmark is a good example of how to manage rivers holistically in the future. The river had been straightened in order to create more farmland. Use the Internet to find out how the Brede is managed today and then write a river report on the Brede. Your report should include how the river was managed in the past and how it is managed today.

Farmland and buildings on the floodplain of the River Nile in Egypt. The flooding of the Nile washes fertile sediment onto the land. But as the river is controlled by dams, fewer floods occur and farmers are forced to use more artificial fertilisers.

HELPING HAND
Log on to: www.therrc.co.uk/projects/
brede.htm for help researching your report
on the River Brede in Denmark.

Coastal defence

The sea and the weather constantly erode cliffs, depositing rock material on to the beaches below. In time the rocks break down into smaller fragments, such as pebbles, and eventually into sand. Many places in coastal areas are being protected by different engineering schemes. It is hoped that these will preserve the coastline for the future.

KEY SKILLS

Interpreting photographs

Analysing information; making predictions

Drawing accurate sketches

HARD ENGINEERING

People who have houses or farmland on the coast want to protect the coastline from erosion. If nothing is done, eventually the land will be washed into the sea. Sea walls, groynes, rock armour and other types of hard engineering schemes are constructed to reduce erosion in one place, but often these cause problems in other places along the coast. If the coastline in some areas is protected, less sand is produced by erosion. This means that beaches are narrower further along the coast. Narrower beaches cannot stop waves as effectively, so erosion actually speeds up where the sea defences stop.

BEACH SKETCH

Look at the picture of groynes below. Find out what other effects groynes have on the coast. Draw a sketch of a beach that is being eroded, such as Pensacola Beach, Florida, USA. What scheme would you use? Look at soft engineering (right). Would you use this instead of a hard engineering solution?

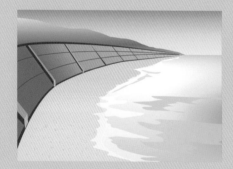

A sea wall
Sea walls are usually made of concrete. They protect the land behind from erosion. Sea walls are expensive to build and only protect the land as far as they extend. They will also erode eventually.

Groynes
Groynes are usually made from wood and extend out towards the sea. They help beach material to build up, which prevents waves from eroding the coastline. Groynes can be expensive to upkeep.

Rock armour
Rock armour is made up of large boulders or blocks of concrete. It reduces the impact of waves and slows down land erosion. It can be difficult to obtain rocks and to get them into position.

The roots of mangrove trees help to hold together the soil and prevent it from being washed away by waves.

SOFT ENGINEERING

Most people agree that hard engineering is not a sustainable solution. Coastlines need to be protected using other schemes, known as soft engineering. One method is to allow the coastline to change without building sea defences, or even to remove existing sea defences in some places, and to restrict building development close to the coast. This policy is called "strategic retreat".

It encourages people to retreat from the threatened areas at the coast by imposing tough planning rules.

Another way is to work with nature to provide natural sea defences. In some areas of Thailand, the Philippines and on the north Australian coast, areas of mangrove forest have been cut down to improve beaches for the tourist industry. The mangrove trees absorb 80% of the energy

from storm waves, so when they are cut down, the coastal areas are at much greater risk of erosion and flooding. Now mangrove forests are being replanted along some coasts and companies are being encouraged to stop cutting down trees. This is a form of sustainable planning as the trees will protect the coastline naturally, without causing any adverse effects.

Forests of the future

Forests are vital to the health of Earth and its people. Trees cover a fifth of all the land on Earth, and help to regulate the gases in the atmosphere, absorbing carbon dioxide and producing oxygen. The roots of trees help prevent the soil from being washed away, while the dead leaves and branches rot down to make the soil fertile so that plants can grow. Forests provide a rich habitat for all types of wildlife.

KEY SKILLS

Looking at a global issue

Completing a spider diagram; writing a report

Researching forests

TYPES OF FOREST

There are many different types of forest around the world. Use the Internet and reference books to find out more about each of the type of forest shown on this map. Find out in which climate the type of forest occurs and what the trees look like – for example, trees in rainforests often have tall trunks, large buttress roots and a canopy of leaves.

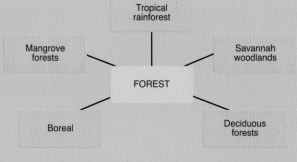

You can display your information on a spider diagram, similar to the one above.

This map shows the current location of the world's major forests.

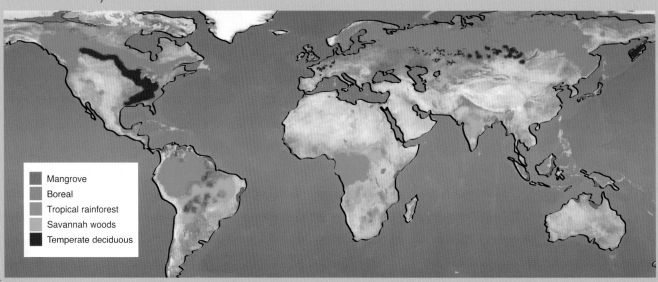

Mangrove
Boreal
Tropical rainforest
Savannah woods
Temperate deciduous

Logging is one of the main contributors to global deforestation.

HELPING HAND

Look at the archive report at: archive.greenpeace.org/comms/cbio/brazil.html and use some of the information in your rainforest report (see below).

DEFORESTATION

Human activity is slowly leading to areas of deforestation around the world as people cut down trees. In South America, an area of rainforest the size of a football pitch is cut down every second. People use the wood as a building material, for furniture and to burn for heating and cooking. Sometimes areas of land are cleared for farmland or for new settlements. The loss of these trees also means the loss of many animals and plants in these areas.

SUSTAINABLE FORESTRY

Many people are working to encourage good forest management worldwide, so that people replant forests and leave some untouched. This is called sustainable forestry and wood that has been grown in this way is marked with a logo, such as the FSC (Forest Stewardship Council) logo. Encourage your family to buy only wood and wooden furniture that carries these marks.

In the state of Acre in Brazil, the government has put into action a plan to use the forests without losing them for ever. Where trees have been cut down, farmers must plant a variety of other trees. Some grow quickly, like banana trees, and others, such as apple and mahogany, take longer. The government knows that it cannot stop all logging and so it allows some in certain areas. The government also makes sure that the logging companies plant new trees to replace those logged. This way there will still be forests on Earth in the future.

RAINFORESTS WRITING

Prepare an extended piece of writing about Brazil and its tropical rainforests. Discuss the various plans people have to use and preserve the rainforests; find out what types of trees are in high demand and which plants and animals are in danger.

How to use energy

Think about your day so far. Have you switched on any lights, listened to the radio, walked to school? All of these activities required energy to make them happen. Eating food gave you the energy to walk to school, while burning fossil fuels in power stations probably provided the electricity needed to power the radio and light your home.

City lights in the centre of Tokyo, Japan. In the future people will have to find other sources of power as fossil fuels run out.

NON-RENEWABLE ENERGY

Most of the energy we use today to power cars, keep houses warm, cook food and make machines work comes from non-renewable energy sources such as fossil fuels. Coal, oil and gas are all fossil fuels, which formed millions of years ago from the fossilised remains of plants and animals. People are using up fossil fuels quickly and eventually they will run out. Fossil fuels also produce pollution when they are burned – pollution that affects the lungs of people on the ground and the balance of gases in Earth's protective atmosphere (see page 20–21).

RENEWABLE ENERGY

Some people think that renewable energy is the answer to our future energy needs. Renewable energy will never run out as it is involves using the energy from the Sun (solar power), wind (wind power), water (hydro-electricity) and plants (biogas) to make electricity. Solar panels absorb heat energy from the Sun and use it to heat up water and generate electricity. Wind power is generated by huge wind turbines located in open spaces. Hydro-electricity is produced by damming a river and then using the trapped water to turn a huge wheel, which generates electricity. Biogas, also called digester gas, is the gas produced by the fermentation of organic matter including manure, wastewater sludge, municipal solid waste, or any other biodegradable feedstock.

A hydro-electric dam on the River Rhine, Germany.

While renewable energy does not cause pollution, it can create other problems. For example, areas of land are flooded for hydro-electricity projects to form reservoirs that store the water before it flows through electricity generators. People lose their homes and land for ever. On a smaller scale, some people object to wind farms because they are often located in areas of natural beauty.

Use the Internet to find out about a dam project that generates renewable energy – for example the Lesotho Highlands Water project. Use the website at www.lhwp.org.ls as a starting point to find out where the project is, what it does, how it affects the local community and how it is working towards a sustainable future. Then, using your ICT skills, design a leaflet to inform other people about the project.

Climate change

Our climate is the average weather we experience over a long period of time. Scientists can show us that there have always been changes in the climate during Earth's long history, and weather records show that some decades were hotter than others. What is new is the speed of climate change today, accompanied by much more extreme weather patterns across the world.

KEY SKILLS

Looking at global issues

Interpreting maps

Doing research

Designing a poster

GLOBAL WARMING

Many scientists think that the world climate is changing because human activity is upsetting the balance of carbon dioxide in Earth's atmosphere. The atmosphere forms a protective blanket around Earth, shielding it from harmful rays from the Sun, while allowing the Sun's heat energy to reach Earth. Levels of some gases, including carbon dioxide (CO_2), in the atmosphere prevent excess heat energy from escaping back into space. Gradually this natural process, called the greenhouse effect, is causing global temperatures to rise more quickly because of pollution in the atmosphere. Changes in Earth's temperature, together with rising sea levels, will have a devastating impact on low-lying countries and many coastal areas and marine habitats.

This illustration shows how the temperature of Earth's surface is rising. Many scientists believe that emissions from factories, traffic, etc are speeding up the process.

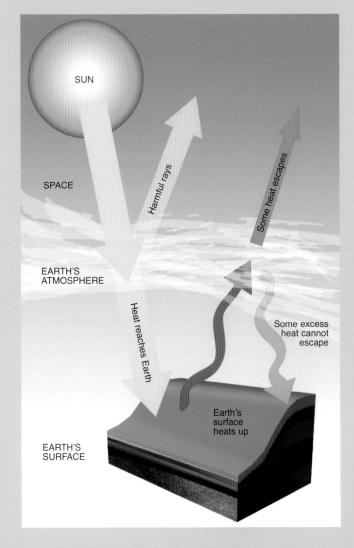

SUN

SPACE

Harmful rays

Some heat escapes

EARTH'S ATMOSPHERE

Heat reaches Earth

Some excess heat cannot escape

Earth's surface heats up

EARTH'S SURFACE

WHAT CAN BE DONE?

On an international level, world leaders have met on several occasions to discuss plans to reduce the speed of climate change. In 1995 at Kyoto, Japan, some governments agreed that only more economically developed countries (MEDCs) should have to cut CO_2 emissions. LEDCs were not required to reduce their CO_2 emissions because they were low at the time.

This illustration shows the different levels of carbon dioxide (CO_2) produced by each country. The greens show the countries with the highest emissions.

Since 1995, the economies of some LEDCs, such as India and China, have grown rapidly, and as a result their CO_2 emissions have risen. Today, the international community feels that these countries should reduce their emissions. In addition, the USA refused to sign the Kyoto agreement despite the fact that it produces high levels of CO_2. So there is still a tremendous amount being pumped into our atmosphere.

Look at the map below to see which countries produce the highest levels of CO_2. Are there most emissions in LEDCs or MEDCs? Why do you think this happens?

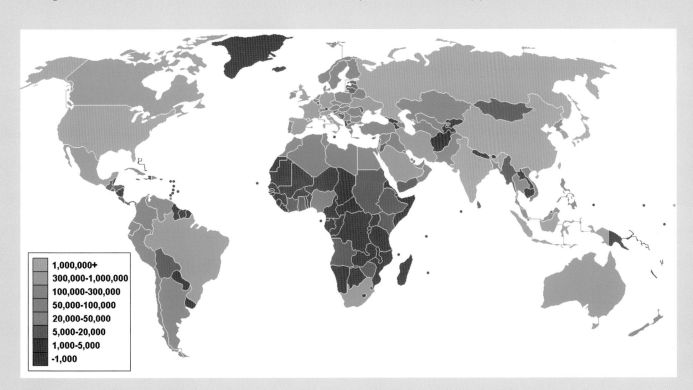

| 1,000,000+ |
| 300,000-1,000,000 |
| 100,000-300,000 |
| 50,000-100,000 |
| 20,000-50,000 |
| 5,000-20,000 |
| 1,000-5,000 |
| -1,000 |

PERSONAL ENERGY PLAN

We can all help to reduce climate change by taking action in our everyday lives. Just remembering to switch off lights, asking parents to use energy-saving light bulbs, wearing more clothes rather than turning up the heating, and turning off computers and televisions rather than leaving them on stand-by will save a lot of energy in a year.

It will also reduce electricity bills! Go to www.globalactionplan.org.uk for many more ideas on how to save energy. Look at their kids' zone. Then use some of your new knowledge to produce your own energy-saving plan. You could also design a striking poster to encourage others to use less energy and therefore slow down climate change. Ask whether you can display the poster in your school.

Earthquakes

Earthquakes are one of the most destructive natural hazards on Earth. They occur at the point where one of the Earth's plates (which form Earth's outer layer) becomes stuck when it slides against another plate. Pressure builds up under Earth's surface until the plate jolts free, causing the ground to move violently – an earthquake. Depending on how many people are living in the area, the earthquake's strength, and the level of economic development, earthquakes can cause loss of life and damage to buildings.

KEY SKILLS

 Doing research

 Writing a report; making comparisons

 Looking at photographs

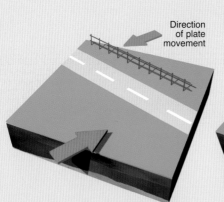

Direction of plate movement

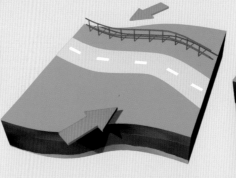

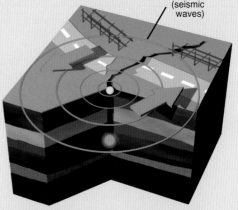

Shockwaves (seismic waves)

This road and fence are built across a fault line. Two of Earth's plates are sliding past each other.

Over time the plates move but they are stuck along the fault line. Pressure builds up underground.

Suddenly, energy is released from underground as the plates jolt free. This point underground is called the focus (the red dot). The movement releases shockwaves – called seismic waves – in all directions. The epicentre (the yellow dot) is directly above at the surface. This is usually where the most damage occurs.

THE SAN FRANCISCO STORY

In 1906 an earthquake in San Francisco, USA, almost completely destroyed the city. About 3,000 people were killed and over half the population of the city (about 225,000 people) were made homeless. It took days to control the fires that broke out all over the city. Yet a strong earthquake in the same city in 1989 caused only 63 deaths, with 3,500 injuries and damage to 100,000 buildings.

RESEARCH AND REPORT

Go to the Internet site of The Virtual Museum of the City of San Francisco at www.sfmuseum.org to read reports of both the 1906 and 1989 earthquakes and see photographs of the damage. Use some of this information to write a report comparing the two earthquakes, highlighting how the city's planning reduced deaths.

CAN PEOPLE BE PROTECTED FROM EARTHQUAKES?

There are some measures that people can take to prepare for earthquakes, but nothing can protect people completely. In MEDCs, such as Japan and the USA, all new buildings and road structures in known earthquake zones are built to strict anti-earthquake standards. These buildings absorb some of the power of the earthquakes. People living in known earthquake zones are encouraged to keep an earthquake pack at home, including a first-aid kit, tinned food and a battery-powered radio. In Japan, people receive earthquake emergency training to reduce panic and deaths. In MEDCs, money is spent on up-to-date monitoring of earthquake zones in order to help predict earthquakes.

The aftermath of the earthquake that rocked San Francisco in 1989. Safety plans helped to save many lives.

HELPING HAND

Earthquake strength is measured by a machine called a seismometer. It produces a graph that shows the strength of Earth's movements. The strength is graded using the Richter Scale, where higher numbers represent the strongest earthquakes.

In LEDCs, buildings are often constructed to lower standards, so they are more likely to collapse during an earthquake. Emergency services are often less able to respond, so it can be days or even weeks before help or emergency supplies reach remote areas. With less money available, it can take a lot longer to rebuild damaged buildings and repair roads and railways.

PAKISTAN EARTHQUAKE IN 2005

Research the earthquake in Pakistan in 2005 and compare it with the information you gathered on the San Francisco earthquake of 1989 in the activity above. Start by logging on to news.bbc.co.uk/1/hi/world/south_asia/4324534.stm and reading the archived news report.

Reduce, reuse, recycle

Many items that we throw away every day could be reused or recycled. Recycling means putting a material, such as glass, paper or metal, through a process so that it can be used again. Reusing products means finding a second use for them, or finding a new owner.

RECYCLE

Recycling products reduces the demand for raw materials and reduces the amount of waste. New York City in the USA produces 34,000 tonnes of rubbish every day, of which 50% is paper that could be recycled. All this waste has to be disposed of to keep the city clean. Some waste is burnt in incinerators; other waste is buried in landfill sites. Once materials such as paper or glass have been disposed of

like this, they are usually lost for ever. By recycling things made of paper and glass, the raw materials locked up inside them are kept in use.

Every tonne of recycled paper prevents approximately 17 trees from being cut down and saves 4,100 kilowatts of electricity – enough to heat the average home for six months.

This paper was collected from homes as part of a local recycling scheme.

PERSONAL ACTION PLAN

There are many ways that we can all reduce, reuse or recycle materials to save resources or relieve pressure on landfill sites. Here are a few ideas:

- Keep paper, cardboard, glass, plastics, textiles and metals separate from other household rubbish. Find out whether these items can be collected from your home or persuade your parents or carers to take them to recycling collection points.
- If you have access to a garden, ask your parents or carers to get a composter and use it to collect vegetable peelings and garden waste. Eventually this will form garden compost to improve the soil in the garden.
- If you live in a house, ask an adult to fit a water butt to the drainpipe and collect rain water. Reuse this on your garden rather than using new water.
- Buy food and other products that have minimum packaging. This way you will not have to throw as much away.
- Take bags to the supermarket, rather than using new bags each time.
- When shopping, buy recycled paper products where possible, including envelopes and writing paper.
- Take unwanted games, household items, books and clothes to charity shops or collection points. These can then be reused by somebody else.
- Mobile phones, printer cartridges, even bicycles, can all be recycled or repaired by people. Log on to www.oxfam.org.uk/ what_you_can_do/recycle to find out how to do this in the UK.

RECYCLING SURVEY

Draw up a table like the one shown below. List ten household waste products (we have started you off) and then survey ten people to find out what they normally do with these particular products. Do they bin them, reuse them or recycle them?

Present your data as a pie chart showing the proportion recycled or reused as against binned. Your pie chart may look something like this:

WASTE PRODUCT	BIN	RECYCLE/REUSE
Apple core and skin		
Empty juice carton		
Old mobile phone		
Old T-shirt		
Empty glass bottle		

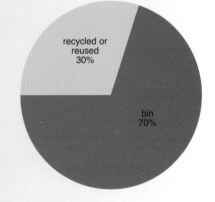

recycled or reused 30%

bin 70%

Overpopulation

Each country has its own resources, such as soil, water, land and minerals, that support the people living there. In countries where the population is high or rising quickly, people are more likely to have a low standard of living, or even be threatened by famine, because there are not enough resources for everyone. Governments create plans to solve the problem of over-population in their country.

FOCUS ON CHINA

During the 20th century, the population of China was growing at an alarming rate. The government of China worried about how they would feed all these people, and announced a "one child policy" in 1979 to slow down the birth rate. This meant that married couples could have only one child by law. The child would receive benefits, such as free education and healthcare, as well as priority housing. A second child would receive no education or healthcare. Look at the two population pyramids for China for 1990 and 2006. Predict how the pyramid will look in 2050. What impact has the policy had on Chinese population growth?

HELPING HAND
The birth rate is the number of babies born each year per 1,000 of the population. The number of deaths each year per 1,000 of the population is called the death rate.

CHINA 1990

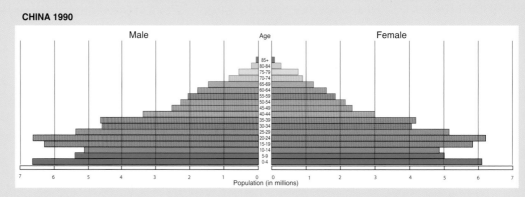

CHINA 2006

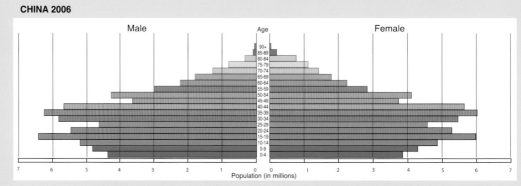

FOCUS ON SOUTHERN INDIA

In Kerala, a state in southern India, the local government decided that education was the best way to reduce birth rates, rather than forced policies. Here, women and girls had to attend school by law, enabling many of them to get better jobs on leaving school. The girls were given sex education to help them plan their families.

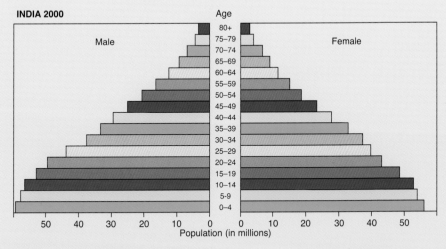

INDIA 2000

Male   Age   Female

80+
75–79
70–74
65–69
60–64
55–59
50–54
45–49
40–44
35–39
30–34
25–29
20–24
15–19
10–14
5-9
0–4

50 40 30 20 10 0   0 10 20 30 40 50
Population (in millions)

Women and children in rural India are given sex education lessons. Many people believe education will help to control birth rates in the future.

Since the start of this scheme, 2,800 villages have formed into "mandals" or community organisations. These mandals run childcare centres, adult literacy classes, welfare services and activities to improve the status of women. All of these encourage women to have fewer babies for positive reasons and today Kerala is not an over-populated state.

Of the two policies looked at, which do you think is the better way to curb over-population? Which policy is more sustainable?

Underpopulation

Underpopulation occurs in countries where the birth rate is falling. As a result, the population of the country gets smaller and there is a higher percentage of old people. Some countries, such as Italy, Japan and Russia, are worried that they will not have enough people in the future to do all the jobs that are necessary for a country to function.

KEY SKILLS

Looking at global issues

Using the Internet

Interpreting information

Looking at population pyramids

The population of many MEDCs will change over the next 30 years. People who live in Japan are waiting longer to have children or not having any at all.

WHY ARE BIRTH RATES DIFFERENT?

The cost of living in some countries, such as Japan, is extremely high. By the time a young couple has paid for housing, food, water and electricity, they may feel that they can afford only to have one child, or none at all. Some women, in particular, may decide not to have children because they are enjoying their career and the lifestyle it brings them. In addition, advances in medicine and a better standard of living mean that many people are living far longer lives than in the past, which leads to an ageing population.

HELPING HAND

Population pyramids also show information about life expectancy. Pyramids in many countries are becoming square as people live longer.

PLANNING FOR FUTURE GENERATIONS

In the way that some countries have formed plans to reduce their populations, others are looking for ways to increase their population. For example, the authorities in the UK, New Zealand and Australia encourage economic migrants to fill the job gaps caused by the countries' falling birth rates. If the country does not have enough teachers or doctors, then teachers and doctors from other countries are given work permits and encouraged to move or migrate. Not everybody agrees with this policy because it leaves the country of origin with fewer doctors and teachers. This process is called "brain drain". In Russia, the government has tried something completely different. They have actively encouraged women to have more babies and offer prizes and rewards for those who do.

COMPARING POPULATION PYRAMIDS

Log on to the following website http://www.census.gov/ipc/www/idbpyr.html to find population pyramids for your country and look at the pyramid below for Japan.

What challenges will Japan face in 30 years' time. How do these challenges compare with those that your country will face? Should people work for longer so that the population is more sustainable? How do these pyramids compare with those for China and India (see pages 26–27)?

JAPAN 2006

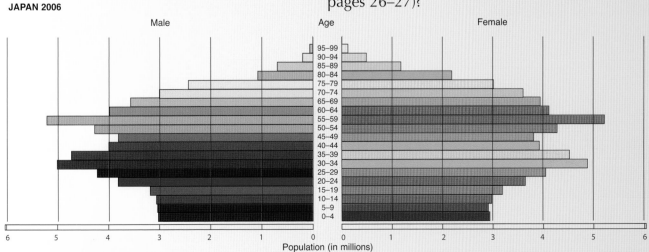

Settlements in the future

The places where people live are called settlements. Settlements are organised into a hierarchy with small hamlets and villages near the bottom and large cities at the top. As countries develop, people migrate to the bigger settlements for work and the chance to improve their standard of living. However, some cities have grown too quickly, leaving some poorer people with low-quality housing and limited services.

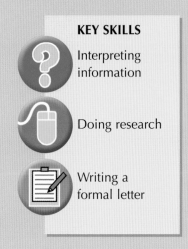

KEY SKILLS

Interpreting information

Doing research

Writing a formal letter

Settlements can be organised in order of their importance to form a settlement hierarchy. There are fewer cities so they are at the top of the pyramid.

CITY

TOWN

VILLAGE

HAMLET

MILLIONAIRE CITIES

Millionaire cities are settlements with over one million residents. There are more than 280 millionaire cities in the world and it is these very large cities that are causing concern for planners as they continue to grow and sprawl out into the surrounding countryside. Some cities, such as Mexico City, Los Angeles and Tokyo, have more than 10 million inhabitants and are given a different name – mega-cities. Other huge cities, such as those on the east coast of the USA, have spread into each other and formed a huge megalopolis stretching from Boston down to Washington D.C. This huge urban area has become known as Boswash.

URBAN PROBLEMS

When places grow rapidly, problems often emerge. In Mexico City, house-building cannot keep up with the rise in population, so people are forced to build homes out of any materials they can find. These slum dwellings gather in areas called favelas, where the standard of living is very poor. Mexico City also has high levels of traffic congestion, leading to poor air quality and difficulty travelling around the city. In addition, 11,000 tonnes of rubbish are created every day, but there are only resources to collect 9,000 tonnes so a lot of rubbish is left in the streets.

SUSTAINABLE DEVELOPMENT

Some countries are looking at ways to allow cities to grow without ruining the area for current residents or future generations. For example, in the UK, town and city planners have created "green belts" around many towns and cities to restrain their growth and preserve green spaces, such as forests and park land. Development in these green spaces is severely restricted.

SUSTAINABLE CITY

Curitiba in Brazil is considered to be one of the most sustainable cities in the world. Many people who live there are happy with their city. The mayor, Jaimie Lerner, was largely responsible for the success of the settlement. He and the other people in power enjoyed solving problems by listening to the city people and keeping solutions small scale and practical. Their rubbish problem was solved by giving poor people money for every bag of rubbish they brought to the recycling centre. The traffic congestion problem was solved by banning cars from most areas and replanting these areas with flowers and grass. The traffic was rerouted into one-way streets with some streets saved for buses. The buses run past the apartment complexes, which encourages residents to use public transport rather than their cars. Favelas still exist, but the city often employs single mothers from these areas in lower-paid roles, and architects help to build homes affordably, one room at a time.

ACTION PLAN

Using Curitiba as a model, can you think of ways that the governers of Mexico City could improve the standard of living for its residents and future residents? Prepare a draft for a letter to the governors of Mexico City, detailing your findings. Remember to use formal language in your letter.

Mexico City, like many large cities, has grown rapidly, and is now facing problems associated with overcrowding and pollution.

HELPING HAND
Find out more about cities at www.un.org/cyberschoolbus/habitat/index.asp – part of the UN cities programme.

Fair trade

If every country in the world had to exist on its own, there would not be very many different things for its population to buy or eat and the country would not be very wealthy. To solve this problem, countries trade with one another. They sell (export) the things that they grow or make and then buy (import) the things that they cannot grow or make.

UNFAIR TRADING

While trading can result in economic growth and employment for people, many trading arrangements are not fair to the producers of goods. For example, because consumers in MEDCs want cheap clothes and clothing companies want big profits, many of the clothes in our shops are made in "sweatshops" in LEDCs where people work long hours for very small wages. Many food products are also grown where the lowest possible wage is paid to the farmer or farm-worker. With few other job opportunities, many families are forced to struggle on in poverty and often cannot afford to educate their children.

A worker tips out cocoa beans on a fair trade farm in Ghana.

FAIR TRADING

One solution to this problem is to encourage fair trading. Fair trade is about paying a fair price to the producer for their product, whether that be bananas, cocoa beans or cotton. In addition, the buyer pays a "social premium" – an extra sum of money – which is used in the producers' community to improve healthcare, education or services. Long-term business relationships are set up between producers and buyers so that farmers know they will have a market for their goods, at a fair and fixed price. There are many examples of fair trade success stories, for example, the chocolate Dubble Bar is made from cocoa grown by farmers in the Kuapa Kokoo co-operative in Ghana, West Africa.

HELPING HAND
Visit www.dubble.co.uk to find out more about the Dubble Bar, Divine fair trade chocolate and the Fairtrade mission.

FAIRTRADE FOOD ACTION PLAN

You may have noticed the Fairtrade logo on the packaging of some of the foods you eat, or that are available in the shops. You can see the logo at www.fairtrade.org.uk and find out more about Fairtrade products. You can help to improve the lifestyles of farmers in LEDCs by choosing foods with this label and persuading others to buy them, too. Sometimes the fair trade food product may be more expensive than the non-fair trade alternative, but it is worth remembering that a much greater proportion of the price of the food has benefited the farmer who grew the food in the first place. Many different foods carry the logo, such as bananas, chocolate, sugar, raisins and honey.

Complete a survey of how many fair trade products a group of ten people buy. You may want to set up a table like the one below, adding other products.

FAIRLY TRADED PRODUCT	NUMBER OF PEOPLE WHO BUY IT
bananas	
coffee	
sugar	
raisins	
chocolate	

Using the data you have collected, draw up a bar chart with the following axes:

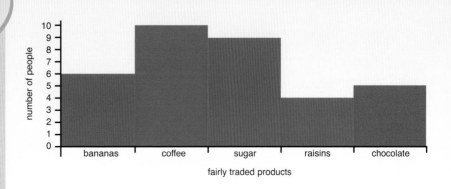

City transport

As places develop and people become wealthier, higher demands are placed on transport. Many roads become congested and air quality deteriorates. Many of the major cities of the world, such as Mexico City, London, Tokyo, Paris and Shanghai, share this problem.

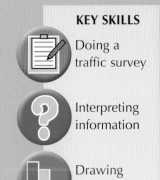
GOING UNDERGROUND

One solution is to build more road and train systems underground. Developers believe these will reduce congestion and improve air quality above ground. The city of Boston, USA, has recently started a massive underground road project, named the "Big Dig", to relieve some of the traffic congestion. Many people believe that more roads only encourage more traffic, and that road building is not a sustainable solution. Many cities, including Paris and New York, have underground train systems which are efficient ways of moving lots of people around. These are expensive, but they provide a good option for city travel in the future.

Part of the underground network, called the Big Dig, in Boston, USA. Developers hope to move some traffic from the overground roads.

RIDING THE BUS

A bus occupies the space of three cars but can carry 40 or more people. If more people used buses, it would reduce the number of cars on the roads. However, when people have experienced slow journeys by bus due to traffic jams, they often prefer to control their journey by travelling by car. To solve this problem, many urban areas have introduced dedicated bus lanes. The buses use these to bypass traffic jams and provide a better alternative to individual car travel.

Bus lanes might encourage people to use buses, but bus travel still has to be affordable. In Bremen, Germany, the price of a bus ticket has been subsidised by the government, making it cheaper to buy. At the same time, in some places such as London, car travel into the city centre has been reduced by introducing a congestion charge – a sum of money that must be paid for entering the city centre.

The monorail in Sydney, Australia is one of many transport schemes built in cities around the world to reduce traffic congestion.

CONDUCT A TRAFFIC SURVEY

With a friend, plan and carry out a traffic survey in your local area to compare how many people use public transport and how many use private cars. Choose the location of the survey – maybe at some traffic lights or a road junction – making sure that you stand in a safe area and can see the traffic clearly. One person counts the number of cars and buses that drive past you, while the other records how many people are in each vehicle (you might have to estimate the number of people on a bus). Write the results on a table like the one below.

Which type of transport was more popular? Use the data from your survey to draw pie charts. The first pie chart should compare the number of vehicles and the second should compare the number of people travelling. What do your results tell you about the two different types of transport?

	number of vehicles	number of people
cars		
buses		

DEVELOPING OTHER FORMS OF TRANSPORT

The city authority of Sydney, Australia has developed a monorail which transports people above existing roads. In Manchester in the UK and San Francisco in the USA, tram networks have been developed to carry people along a set route.

Controlling tourism

Tourism is the fastest growing industry and creates many jobs. It employs about 10% of all people of working age worldwide, although many of these jobs are low paid and part-time. Sometimes too many tourists can cause problems for the places they visit, and travelling vast distances by aeroplane or car causes pollution. Sustainable plans must be made to ensure the planet survives for future generations.

KEY SKILLS

Designing a hotel; drawing a sketch map

Doing research

Interpreting information

Tourists fill a beach in Mallorca. Increasing numbers of people are able to afford holidays abroad.

FAIR TOURISM

Fair tourism is about looking after staff and using as many local resources and services as possible in the tourist industry. The Backpack Hostel in Cape Town, South Africa is a perfect example of this. The profits from the hostel are shared with the community, for example, a crèche has been built for small children to attend while their parents work. As much food as possible is bought from local farmers, and local people are employed and involved in the running of the hostel. Local artists display and sell their work in the hostel, too. The result is that local people benefit from tourism and are treated fairly.

This hut is part of an eco-tourism project in South Africa.

ECO-TOURISM

Eco-tourism aims to generate money and create jobs for local people, while protecting the local environment and culture in a sustainable way. In 2003, the community of Piedra Blanca in Ecuador decided to try to improve its economic situation by developing an eco-tourism project. Visitors stay in the village, paying villagers for accommodation. Local guides have been fully trained and take it in turns to accompany the tourists. This allows all guides to earn money from the tourists. There are strict rules to protect the people's culture as well. For example, tourists must wear suitable clothing and obey the rules of the forest. The money that the villagers make allows them to carry out local conservation and reforestation schemes.

WHAT CAN YOU DO?

Flying is a quick way to reach your holiday destination. However, aeroplanes are huge polluters and flying increases your "eco footprint" (see page 9). When you go on holiday, remember to eat local food where possible and look out for fair tourism or eco-tourism trips.

DESIGN A HOTEL

Use the Internet and the information you have learnt so far to design an eco-friendly hotel. Before you start designing the building, think about the following:

- What materials will be used to build the hotel?
- What type of power will you use in the hotel?
- Who will run the hotel?
- How will the profits be used?
- Where will the food come from?

Once you have decided on these factors, draw a sketch map of the hotel annotating the sustainable features.

Our food

Forty years ago, most people's everyday diet was made up of food grown and sold locally. Today, some foods are transported thousands of kilometres to our shops using air transport or shipping, which is causing environmental problems. Also, in some cases, food resources are being exploited in a way that is not sustainable. For example, over-fishing in one area causes fish stocks to get so low that there may not be enough fish for people in the future.

KEY SKILLS

Keeping a food diary

Looking at food labels

Cargo is unloaded from a plane. Food is transported to our shops from all around the world.

Demands on fish stocks mean that quotas may get even smaller in future.

FOOD TRANSPORTATION

Transporting food contributes to climate change because fossil fuels power planes and lorries. People are now calculating the distance food is transported to reach our shops. For example, an apple grown in New Zealand travels approximately 36,700 kilometres to reach shops in the UK, whereas a locally grown variety may only have travelled a few kilometres. Eating food that is in season locally can reduce this figure.

FISHING QUOTAS AND MARINE RESERVES

To prevent over-fishing, quotas can be set to limit the amount of fish that can be caught in a particular area each year. An alternative is to establish marine reserves. This has been done successfully around Australia, where young fish can now grow to full size in the protected marine reserves and then be released. In this way, there is always a new stock of fish growing for the next generation.

SUSTAINABLE FARMING

After World War II (1939–45), farmers in the UK were encouraged to produce more food and this led to intensive farming practices. Wetlands were drained, hedgerows removed and the use of chemical fertilisers and pesticides became widespread. All of this has harmed the environment. Greater priority is now being given to encouraging farmers to use sustainable methods. These include using less fertiliser, or using natural fertilisers, and introducing certain insects to keep pests under control. Some farmers now farm organically or without pesticides.

THINK GLOBAL, ACT LOCAL

Keep a food diary for a week, recording everything you eat and where it came from, where possible. At the end of the week, look at what you have eaten and try to come up with seasonal or more local alternatives to the food that has travelled the furthest.

Breaking out of poverty

If the world were a village of 100 people, the richest person would have more wealth than the poorest 57 combined. The poorest people are said to be in poverty. There are two types of poverty – relative and absolute. Relative poverty is when people cannot afford to buy luxuries, such as a computer. Although life might be a struggle, conditions are not life-threatening. Absolute poverty is when life itself is threatened. In absolute poverty a person may receive no education, be unable to afford decent housing, or enough food, and may not have access to clean drinking water.

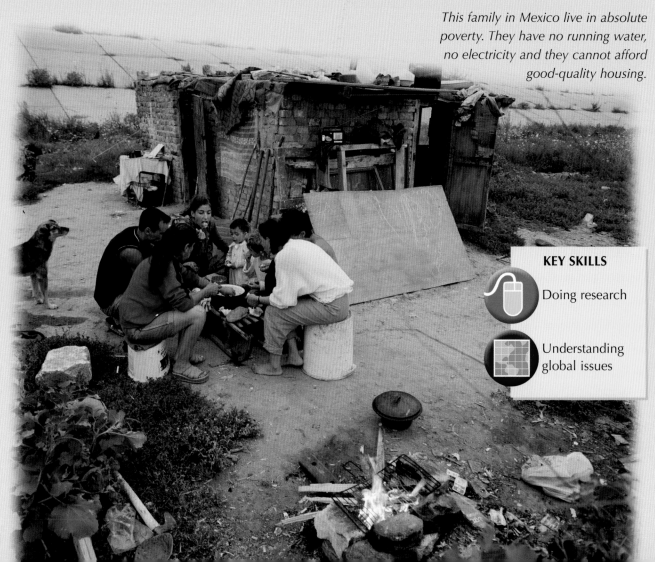

This family in Mexico live in absolute poverty. They have no running water, no electricity and they cannot afford good-quality housing.

KEY SKILLS

Doing research

Understanding global issues

CISIRA, SOUTH AFRICA

Imagine Cisira, a small village in eastern Cape Province, South Africa. There is no running water and the 400 people who live there have to drink dirty water from the river. As a result, they get ill but cannot afford to go to the doctor for medicine, as healthcare has to be paid for. Now that they are ill, they cannot go to work, so they do not earn any money. This means that less food can be bought and so it is more difficult to recover. The children cannot go to school, so they do not get an education and as a result they will not be able to get a well-paid job. This is known as the cycle of poverty and it is very difficult to break. There is one way to avoid drinking the dirty water, and that is to buy bottled water from a local supplier. Most people cannot afford to buy bottled water.

HELPING THE PEOPLE OF CISIRA

There is a sustainable solution. "Water for the people" is a scheme that has improved access to clean water for two million people in Africa. Thanks to Ondeo Services, Cisira now has pipes connecting the village to a clean water supply. The residents can buy water at the standpipe using special smart cards. The water costs up to 40% less than bottled water. To get the pipes in place, trenches had to be dug and pipes installed. Most of these jobs went to local people, which meant that they earned money to spend on their children's education and to buy more food. They now have a chance to escape the cycle of poverty.

SEND-A-GOAT!

In Kenya, 55,000 people have escaped poverty as a result of a different project, called Farm Friends, run by Farm Africa. To find out how this scheme works, go to Farm Africa's website: www.farmafrica.org.uk and click on their Farm Friends section. When you have learnt all about it, ask your parents, carers or teacher if they would like to become involved. Perhaps you and your friends could decide not to send Christmas cards this year, but collect the money together to buy a farm animal instead. Your school could run a charity fund-raising event, like a non-uniform day, to buy goats or other farm animals through the Farm Friends scheme.

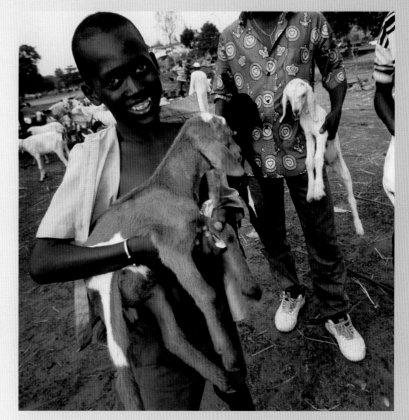

Goats are very important in many African countries. They produce milk and can be sold for money, or slaughtered for their meat.

Reducing the digital divide

If the world were a village of a 100 people, 80 of them would never have heard a telephone dial tone, or have used a computer. The difference between those that have telecommunications technology and those that do not is called the digital divide. It is generally thought that those groups of people without access to technology will fall further and further behind those that do, suffering a much poorer standard of living. Some attempts are being made to solve this problem for the future.

KEY SKILLS

Looking at global issues

Doing research

Completing a report

HEALTHNET

In many places health workers are unable to keep in contact with other people, or keep up-to-date with the latest information on how to treat illnesses. HealthNet is helping to reduce the digital divide by putting those people working in remote areas in contact with other health workers. There is no need for telephone lines because satellite communications are used to reach the most inaccessible areas.

A health worker in rural Gambia can take a picture with a digital camera to record a patient's symptoms. These pictures are then sent to a nearby town where a doctor can help to diagnose the illness. The patient can then be treated and, hopefully, recover.

This doctor is talking to a health worker via satellite link. New technology is helping to reduce the digital divide.

GRAMEENPHONE

In Bangladesh, a mobile phone company is pioneering the "Village Phone" programme. By giving small loans to people to buy mobile phones, it helps the poorest people to earn a living. Jamirum lives in a small village an hour's drive from the capital, Dhaka. She bought a phone through this project. Her phone is the only one in a four-village area where 3,500 people live. Jamirum charges people a small amount to use her phone and makes a profit of about £70 a month – nearly four times the average wage in Bangladesh. Using the phone means that people can stay in touch with relatives who live in other towns or abroad. Farmers can get the local weather report and check prices for their crops. The phones can also be used to give people advanced notice of cyclones. With this information, they can reach safety in time.

This woman in Ghana, Africa is using a satellite mobile phone to talk to her relatives. A phone like this one can connect people in rural areas.

RESEARCH AND REPORT

Use the Internet to research the digital divide in India – a country with a booming telecommunications industry in some places, such as Bangalore, but where many villagers have never used computers or mobile phones. You could start by looking at www.newsbbc.co.uk and then type "digital divide India" into the search box. Use the information to write a report comparing the different experiences of telecommunications in India.

Glossary

Absolute poverty
When people lack the basic things needed to survive, such as food, shelter and clean drinking water.

Atmosphere
The mixture of gases that surrounds the Earth.

Biodegradable
Describing a substance that breaks down, or decomposes, naturally.

Birth rate
The number of people born each year, per thousand population.

Carbon dioxide (CO₂)
An invisible gas found naturally in air. It is released when fossil fuels are burned and is one of the biggest contributers to global warming.

Climate
The average weather conditions of a certain area.

Climate change
A general change in climate that may be due to natural causes, or the effects of human activity in the form of pollution and global warming.

Death rate
Also called mortality rate. The number of people who die each year, per thousand population.

Deforestation
The destruction of forests for building or farming, or to make use of the wood.

Drainage basin
The area of land that is drained by a river system.

Eco footprint
The estimated area of land and sea affected by a single person's lifestyle, measured in global hectares.

Epicentre
The point on the Earth's surface directly above the focus of an earthquake.

Erosion
The loosening of weathered material by the wind, water or ice.

Fair trade
Trading to ensure that a product's producers, such as cocoa farmers or cotton pickers, benefit from its sale.

Floodplain
The wide, flat valley floor characteristic of the lower course of a river, which is often flooded by river water.

Global warming
A gradual increase in the average temperature of the Earth's atmosphere.

Green belt
A strip of protected park or farmland at the boundary of a settlement, designed to prevent urban sprawl.

Greenhouse gases
Gases that trap heat in the Earth's atmosphere.

Groynes
Fence-like structures on a beach which trap material and increase beach depth.

Habitat
The environment where a plant or an animal usually grows or lives.

Hard engineering
Structures to control geographical processes, such as flooding or coastal erosion.

Holistic planning
Considering the sustainable care of, for example, a river, in terms of the whole thing rather than its individual parts.

Intensive farming
Farming to produce maximum crop or animal yields from a limited area of land.

Less economically developed country (LEDC)
A country in which the majority of the population lives in poverty. These countries tend to be mainly rural, but often their cities are growing fast.

Life expectancy
The expected lifespan of a person, measured in years and often taken as an average across a population.

Logging
The removal of trees from a forest to be sold for timber.

More economically developed country (MEDC)
A country with much greater wealth per person and more developed industry than a less economically developed country.

Quota
A limited amount imposed on something, for example the number of fish allowed to be caught in an area of water.

Rural
In the countryside.

Soft engineering
Using natural environmental processes to cope with geographical problems, such a flooding or coastal erosion.

Sustainability
The ability to meet the needs of people and environments today and to maintain them in the future.

Urban
In towns and cities.

Weblinks

www.earthsummit.info
This website contains many weblinks for you to find out more about sustainable development.

www.unesco.org/water
The 'water page' of the United Nations Educational, Scientific and Cultural Organization.

www.nilebasin.org/nilemap.htm
Webpage of the Nile Basin Initiative showing a map of the River Nile. It also has links to other pages about the River Nile.

www.worldlandtrust.org
Website of this wildlife action group that is campaigning to save habitats, including forests, across the world.

www.foei.org
Homepage of Friends of the Earth International, featuring lots of up-to-date news about their environmental campaigns.

www.greenpeace.org/international
The Greenpeace International website which includes climate change and deforestation campaign news.

www.iiees.ac.ir/english/index_e.asp
English language version of the International Institute of Earthquake Engineering and Seismology.

www.overpopulation.org
Website of World Population Awareness, featuring lots of information about why population matters to our future.

Note to parents and teachers:

Every effort has been made by the Publishers to ensure that these websites are suitable for children, that they are of the highest educational value, and that they contain no inappropriate or offensive material. However, because of the nature of the Internet, it is impossible to guarantee that the contents of these sites will not be altered. We strongly advise that Internet access is supervised by a responsible adult.

Index

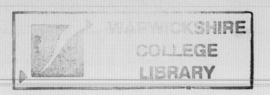